M000036050

A Guide for Using

Harriet the Spy

in the Classroom

Based on the novel written by Louise Fitzhugh

This guide written by Dona Herweck Rice

Teacher Created Materials, Inc.
6421 Industry Way
Westminster, CA 92683
www.teachercreated.com
©1996 Teacher Created Materials, Inc.
Reprinted, 2001
Made in U.S.A.
ISBN 1-57690-133-5

Edited by
Ellen Woodward

Illustrated by
Jose Tapia

Cover Art by
Wendy Chang

T 20827

Table of Contents

Introduction

A good book can touch our lives like a good friend. Within its pages are words and characters that can inspire us to achieve our highest ideals. We can turn to it for companionship, recreation, comfort, and guidance. It can also give us a cherished story to hold in our hearts forever.

In *Literature Units,* great care has been taken to select books that are sure to become good friends!

Teachers who use this literature unit will find the following features to supplement their own valuable ideas.

- Sample Lesson Plans
- Pre-reading Activities
- Biographical Sketch and Picture of the Author
- Book Summary
- Vocabulary Lists and Vocabulary Activity Ideas
- Chapters grouped for study with each section including
    - *a quiz*
    - *a hands-on project*
    - *a cooperative learning activity*
    - *a cross-curricular activity*
    - *an extension into the reader's life*
- Post-reading Activities
- Book Report Ideas
- Research Ideas
- Culminating Activity
- Three Unit Test Options
- Answer Key

We are confident that this unit will be a valuable addition to your planning, and we hope that as you use our ideas, your students will increase the circle of "friends" they have in books.

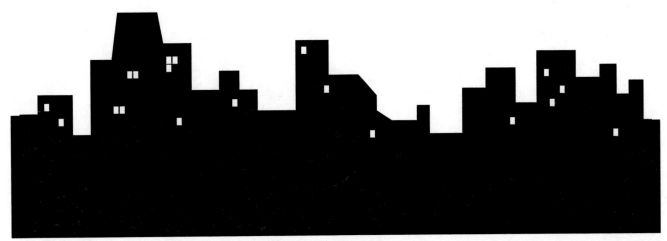

Sample Lesson Plan

Each of the lessons suggested below can take from one to several days to complete.

LESSON 1
- ❖ Introduce and complete some or all of the pre-reading activities found on page 5.
- ❖ Read "About the Author" with your students (page 6).
- ❖ Read the book summary with your students (page 7).
- ❖ Introduce the vocabulary list for Section 1 (page 8).
- ❖ Introduce "Reading Response Journals" (page 10).

LESSON 2
- ❖ Read chapters 1 through 3. As you read, place the vocabulary words in the context of the story and discuss their meanings.
- ❖ Do a vocabulary activity (page 9).
- ❖ Collect, construct, and use spy equipment (page 12).
- ❖ Plan and design an imaginary town (page 13).
- ❖ Discuss the book in terms of geography, working with a map of Manhattan (page 14).
- ❖ Complete the "My Day" activity (page 15).
- ❖ Administer the Section 1 quiz (page 11).
- ❖ Introduce the vocabulary list for Section 2 (page 8).

LESSON 3
- ❖ Read chapters 4 through 6. Place the vocabulary words in context and discuss their meanings.
- ❖ Do a vocabulary activity (page 9).
- ❖ Make a birdcage (page 17).
- ❖ Put together a group recipe book for eggs (page 18).
- ❖ Discuss the book in terms of chemistry, completing a chemical experiment (page 19).
- ❖ Ask the students to describe their own "Ole Golly" (page 20).
- ❖ Administer the Section 2 quiz (page 16).
- ❖ Introduce the vocabulary list for Section 3 (page 8).

LESSON 4
- ❖ Read chapters 7 through 9. Place the vocabulary words in context and discuss their meanings.
- ❖ Do a vocabulary activity (page 9).
- ❖ Portray inanimate objects (page 22).
- ❖ Create a class pageant (page 23).
- ❖ Discuss the book in terms of biology, labeling and coloring parts of the brain (page 24).
- ❖ Ask the students to consider the choices they have in their own lives (page 25).

- ❖ Administer the Section 3 quiz (page 21).
- ❖ Introduce the vocabulary list for Section 4 (page 8).

LESSON 5
- ❖ Read chapters 10 through 12. Place the vocabulary words in context and discuss their meanings.
- ❖ Do a vocabulary activity (page 9).
- ❖ Make a cake from scratch (page 27).
- ❖ Build a class or small group clubhouse (page 28).
- ❖ Discuss the book in terms of math, doing problems that pertain to Harriet (page 29).
- ❖ Ask the students to write a memory (page 30).
- ❖ Administer the Section 4 quiz (page 26).
- ❖ Introduce the vocabulary list for Section 5 (page 8).

LESSON 6
- ❖ Read chapters 13 through 16. Place the vocabulary words in context and discuss their meanings.
- ❖ Do a vocabulary vctivity (page 9).
- ❖ Practice developing empathy for others through mirror imaging (page 32).
- ❖ Develop a class project for community outreach (page 33).
- ❖ Discuss the book in terms of language arts, writing class newspaper pages (page 34).
- ❖ Ask the students to keep a notebook like Harriet's for one week (page 35).
- ❖ Administer the Section 5 quiz (page 31).

LESSON 7
- ❖ Discuss any questions your students may have about the book (page 36).
- ❖ Assign book report and research topics (pages 37 and 38).
- ❖ Begin work on the culminating activity (pages 39–43).

LESSON 8
- ❖ Administer unit tests 1, 2, and/or 3 (pages 44, 45, and 46).
- ❖ Discuss the test answers and responses.
- ❖ Discuss the students' opinions and enjoyment of the book.
- ❖ Continue work on the culminating activity (pages 39–43).

LESSON 9
- ❖ Complete work on the culminating activity (pages 39–43). Share the results.

Before the Book

Before you begin reading *Harriet the Spy*, complete some of the following discussions and activities. This will help provide a strong framework for student interest and involvement in the book.

1. Predict what the story might be about by hearing the title.

2. Predict what the story might be about by looking at the cover illustration.

3. Learn about spies and what they do. Have the students suggest what they might do if they were going to spy.

4. Ask the students to share their opinions about the ethics of spying, both in general and under various conditions or circumstances.

5. Brainstorm for all the occupations that involve spying.

6. Invite a private detective or other professional spy as a guest speaker.

7. Ask the students to share their opinions about baby-sitters, governesses, and caretakers of other kinds who watch over children in place of their parents. Discuss the pros and cons. Allow the students to share their own experiences, if they so choose.

8. Look at a map of North America and find New York. Ask any students who have been to New York, particularly Manhattan, to share their experiences and feelings about what they saw there.

9. This novel was first published in 1964. As a class, do some research into that year and the ways in which things were done in comparison to the current year. For example, compare homes and the ways people lived, the education system, opinions about daycare, and so forth.

10. Invite a guest speaker who remembers 1964 from personal experience. Have the students prepare questions to ask the speaker ahead of time.

11. Have the students answer these questions.

Would you ever. . .

. . . spy on a family member?

. . . spy on a relative or friend?

. . . spy on a stranger in his or her home?

. . . make judgments about people based on what you see and hear?

. . . keep written records of your judgments about people?

. . . spread rumors or gossip about your friends? about strangers?

About the Author

Louise Perkins Fitzhugh was born in Memphis, Tennessee, on October 5, 1928, the daughter of Millsaps, an attorney, and Louise, a homemaker. She attended the Hutchinson School, Southwestern College, Florida Southern College, Bard College, and New York University, studying literature and education.

Six months before completing her degree in literature, Ms. Fitzhugh left school to study art in Italy. She studied at the Art Students League in Italy and later at Cooper Union in New York. Over time, her oil paintings were exhibited in several galleries, where she was known for her realism.

This realism translated to her books for children, most of which were self-illustrated. Ms. Fitzhugh's first book, *Suzuki Beane,* was co-written by Sandra Scoppettone and published in 1961. Its humorous illustrations caught the public eye. From there, she went on to write and publish her most famous and honored book, *Harriet the Spy,* in 1964. However, when the novel was first released, it was met with mixed reviews. Many heralded its "new realism," claiming it as a milestone in children's literature. Others shunned it for this same realism, calling it cynical and sometimes expressing fear that children might take up Harriet's habit of eavesdropping. They also balked at the hypocrisies shown by adults throughout the novel. Despite the scattered negative press, the book became an ALA Notable Book, was on the *New York Times* Outstanding Books of the Year list in 1964, and received the Sequoyah Children's Book Award in 1967. It continues to be read avidly and in 1996, thirty-two years after its publication, was made into a major Hollywood motion picture.

Ms. Fitzhugh continued to publish children's literature, following *Harriet the Spy* with its sequel, *The Long Secret,* in 1965. *Bang, Bang, You're Dead,* an antiwar novel, was co-written by Sandra Scoppettone and published in 1969. Then, after completing her novel *Nobody's Family Is Going to Change,* Louise Fitzhugh died suddenly from an aneurysm on November 19, 1974, at the age of forty-six. Her novel was published posthumously, and then in 1978, it was adapted for television in the NBC production entitled *The Tap Dance Kid.* Broadway recreated *The Tap Dance Kid* in 1983, and it won two Tony Awards. The story tells of a black, upper-middle-class family in New York. The two children, Emma and Willie, aspire to careers considered unacceptable by their parents. Emma wishes to be an attorney, and Willie longs to be a dancer, but their parents consider the first profession to be for men and the latter only suited to women. The book, like *Harriet the Spy,* is noted for its humor and its understanding portrayal of children.

Upon her death, Louise Fitzhugh was working on the text and illustrations for a new children's series. The first book, *I Am Five,* was published in 1978. *I Am Three,* illustrated by Susanna Natti, was published in 1979, and *I Am Four,* illustrated by Susan Bonners, was published in 1982. Another book, *Sport,* was also published in 1979.

In addition to art and writing, Ms. Fitzhugh enjoyed tennis and playing the flute. She lived her life in her home in Bridgewater, Connecticut, and she will always be remembered, as the *New York Times Book Review* once said, as "one of the brightest stars" in children's literature.

Harriet the Spy

by Louise Fitzhugh

(HarperCollins, 1964)

(Available in Canada and UK from HarperCollins Pub. Ltd., and in Australia from HarperCollins)

Harriet is an intelligent, curious, and very observant eleven-year-old girl living in an upper-class Manhattan neighborhood with her father, mother, nurse, and the family cook. She attends a private school, where she closely watches her fellow students and teachers. Each day after school, she makes her rounds on her own spy circuit.

While spying on the people around her, Harriet records her observations in the notebook she carries with her at all times. She fills its pages with her every thought, feeling, and insight.

Harriet has two very dear friends with whom she spends a great deal of time. They are Sport Rocque and Janie Gibbs, both classmates and neighbors. Yet the closest person in the world to Harriet is her nurse, whom she calls Ole Golly. Ole Golly has taken care of Harriet for as long as she can remember. She is Harriet's guide and teacher, and she is keenly aware of Harriet's needs and thoughts.

Ole Golly is a source of great interest to Harriet, so naturally her curiosity is aroused when she learns that Ole Golly has a boyfriend. But then tragedy strikes for Harriet—Ole Golly moves away to marry her boyfriend. Suddenly the house feels empty and Harriet feels alone.

The little spy continues on as best she can, keeping her regular spy route and taking part in class activities. But then the next tragedy happens. Harriet's notebook, filled with disparaging comments about all her classmates, is found and read by all of them.

The entire group shuns her, and the internal anger and emptiness that started with Ole Golly's departure grows every day. She begins to fall behind in school, and she breaks into frequent temper tantrums.

Not knowing what else to do, Harriet's parents take her to a therapist who soon discovers the source of Harriet's trouble, as well as Harriet's needs. Ole Golly is called upon, and she sends a special letter to Harriet, telling her exactly what she needs to hear.

Harriet returns to school, where her parents have taken action that will allow Harriet's great talent for observation and writing to be put to use and nurtured.

Best of all, by following Ole Golly's advice, Harriet is able to apologize to her classmates and become friends once more with Janie and Sport. All is well with the world!

Vocabulary Lists

On this page are vocabulary lists which correspond to each sectional grouping of chapters, as outlined in the table of contents (page 2). Vocabulary activity ideas can be found on page 9 of this book.

SECTION 1: *Chapters 1–3*

apprehensive	egg cream	pompously
arrogantly	gratified	rapping
billowy	hoisted	scowled
brownstone	hypnotized	sedately
careened	intoned	singsong
christened	ledgers	smug
courtyard	loathe	sneer
decisively	motto	tweed
divine	perceive	undercurrent
donning	plaintively	vantage

SECTION 2: *Chapters 4–6*

absolution	eccentric	peevishly
amicable	enigma	profusely
anticlimactic	enunciated	pronouncement
aroused	esplanade	resolutely
bemused	foyer	reverie
colloquy	guerrilla	sedately
complacency	indefinably	tentatively
cretin	ingratiating	uncompromising
disconcerted	minarets	Victorian
duplex	ominous	ward

SECTION 3: *Chapters 7–9*

akin	firmament	petulantly
allotted	flourish	primly
array	gaped	quavered
barrage	gingerly	querulous
conception	horn-rimmed	scallion
cursory	imperiously	sidled
dejectedly	impudence	sotto voce
disgruntled	jowls	treachery
excelsior	newel post	tulle
falsetto	pandemonium	wispy

SECTION 4: *Chapters 10–12*

aghast	dossiers	pivoted
banshee	droned	prism
cabanas	grandeur	semblance
catapulted	grating	signifying
clamoring	jumper	sodden
constitute	listless	spluttered
dawdle	memoirs	stealthily
delusions	menacing	stethoscope
despondently	parquet	wrest
detained	penetrate	zeal

SECTION 5: *Chapters 13–16*

amass	elicit	musing
archly	ensuing	niche
audibly	forlornly	parapet
batty	frisked	prone
bedlam	fuming	regression
chic	hypocrite	retraction
commenced	interjected	reverently
contorting	jubilant	spinet
copious	knots	surreptitiously
disdainfully	languished	virtuous

Vocabulary Activity Ideas

Each chapter section contains several advanced vocabulary words. You may wish to divide the words and assign them to small groups of students. The groups may define the words, find them in the context of the book, and present the information to the class to record in a vocabulary notebook.

You can help your students to learn and retain the vocabulary in *Harriet the Spy* by providing them with interesting vocabulary ideas. Here are a few ideas to try.

- ❐ Ask your students to make their own **Crossword** or **Word Search Puzzles,** using the vocabulary words from the novel.

- ❐ Challenge your students to a **Vocabulary Bee.** This is similar to a spelling bee, but in addition to spelling each word correctly, the game participants must correctly define the words.

- ❐ Play **Vocabulary Concentration.** The goal of this game is to match vocabulary words with their definitions. Divide the class into groups of two to five students. Have the students make two sets of cards the same size and color. On one set, have them write the vocabulary words. On the second set, have them write the definitions. All cards are mixed together and placed facedown on a table. A player picks two cards. If the pair matches the word with its definition, the player keeps the cards and takes another turn. If the cards do not match, they are returned to their places facedown on the table, and another player takes a turn. Players must concentrate to remember the locations of words and definitions. The game continues until all matches have been made. This is an ideal activity for free exploration time.

- ❐ Have your students practice their writing skills by creating sentences and paragraphs in which multiple vocabulary words are used correctly. Ask them to share their **Compact Vocabulary** sentences and paragraphs with the class.

- ❐ Challenge your students to use vocabulary words from the story at least **Ten Times in One Day.** They must keep a record of when, how, and why the word was used.

- ❐ As a group activity, have students work together to create an **Illustrated Dictionary** of the vocabulary words.

- ❐ Play **20 Clues** with the entire class. In this game, one student selects a vocabulary word and gives clues about the word, one by one, until someone in the class can guess the word.

- ❐ Play **Vocabulary Charades.** In this game, vocabulary words are acted out while others guess the word.

- ❐ **Fictionary** can be played as a way of introducing new vocabulary. Establish small groups of four to seven people. You will need note paper of uniform size and color. Someone in the group becomes "It." That person writes down the correct definition of a word from the dictionary on a slip of paper plus a fictional definition on another slip of paper. The other group members then make up their own fictional definitions and write them on slips of paper. Try to make all the definitions sound authentic. "It" collects and shuffles all the definitions and then reads them to the other members. Each, in turn, tries to guess the correct definition. "It" receives one point for each group member successfully "stumped," while the group members who choose correctly each get a point. Play then moves to the next person to the left to be "It."

You probably have many more ideas to add to this list. Try them! Practicing selected words through these types of activities increases student interest in, and retention of, vocabulary.

Reading Response Journals

As your students read *Harriet the Spy*, have them keep *Reading Response Journals. Reading Response Journals* are a wonderful way for students to make personal connections with the literature. In these journals, students can be encouraged to respond to the story in a number of ways. Here are a few ideas:

- Tell the students that the purpose of the journal is to record their thoughts, ideas, observations, and questions as they read the book.

- Provide students with, or ask them to suggest, topics from the story that may stimulate writing. For example, from the chapters in Section 1 you might ask questions such as the following:

    — Why do you think Harriet has such a desire to know everything?

    — Have you ever had an insatiable curiosity such as Harriet's?

- After the reading of each chapter, students can write one or more new things they learned.

- Ask the students to draw their responses to certain events or characters in the story.

- Suggest to your students that they write diary-type responses to their reading by selecting a character and describing events from the character's point of view.

- Encourage students to bring their journal ideas to life by using them to create plays, stories, songs, art displays, and debates.

- Allow students time to write in their journals daily. To evaluate the journals, you may wish to use the following guidelines.

    — Personal reflections will be read by the teacher, but no corrections or letter grades will be assigned. Credit is given for effort, and all students who sincerely try will be awarded credit. If a grade is desired for this type of entry, grade according to the number of journal entries completed. For example, if five journal assignments were made and the student conscientiously completed all five, he or she should receive a letter grade of "A."

    — Nonjudgmental teacher responses should be made as you read the journals to let the students know that you are reading and enjoying their writing. Use comments that will please your journal writers and encourage them to write more. Some possibilities are "You have made me feel as though I were there," or "You have really found what is important in this story."

Quiz Time

1. On the back of this page, list three major events from this section of the book.

2. On the back of this paper, describe Harriet.

3. On the back of this paper, describe Ole Golly.

4. In what city does Harriet live? _____

5. What does Harriet want to do for her career? What is she doing in order to be ready for that career?

   _____

   _____

6. What does Sport want to do for his career? What is his backup choice?

   _____

   _____

7. Ole Golly tells Harriet, "It won't do you a bit of good to know everything if you don't do anything with it." What do you think she means by this?

   _____

   _____

   _____

8. How does Ole Golly feel about her mother? Why do you think so?

   _____

   _____

   _____

9. Who is Mrs. Plumber? Name three things Harriet observes about her.

   _____

   _____

   _____

10. Why do you think Harriet feels "funny watching the scene" of Little Joe giving food to the children?

    _____

    _____

I Spy

In order to spy, Harriet will use whatever materials she has available. As a class, brainstorm for all the materials you might use in order to spy. Make a class master list and, if possible, bring in as many of those supplies as you can.

One particularly interesting piece of equipment that Harriet uses is a dumbwaiter. A dumbwaiter is a small elevator used in homes to carry food and goods from floor to floor. It is usually built on a pulley system, and it has a sliding door in the wall of each floor on which it can make a stop.

To the right is an illustration of a dumbwaiter. The class will divide into groups, and each group will construct its own model of a dumbwaiter based on this illustration.

Materials:

- cardboard
- duct tape or masking tape
- scissors
- craft knife (with adult supervision)
- rope or string
- pulleys

Construction Guidelines:

1. The goal is to make each dumbwaiter as sturdy as possible.

2. Dumbwaiters must be at least 2' (.6 m) wide and 3' (.9 m) high but no larger than 3' (.9 m) wide and 4' (1.2 m) high.

3. Each dumbwaiter can be hoisted over any sturdy overhang that can hold weight easily, such as playground monkey bars.

4. When all the dumbwaiters have been constructed, hold a class contest to see which dumbwaiter is the sturdiest and can hold the most weight. Can any hold a child of about Harriet's size? **Note:** To avoid possible injuries, do not lift children too far off the ground.

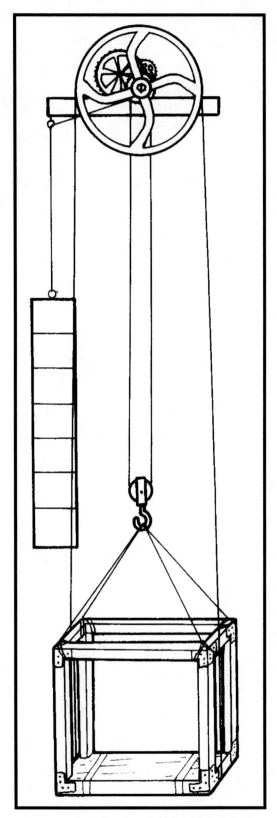

Our Town

Harriet uses her imagination and bits of earth and plant life to create a fictional town and its inhabitants. She even imagines what they are doing, all in the space of a few minutes one night.

Divide into classroom teams. Each team will construct a fictional town, such as Harriet does. However, while Harriet uses only her imagination, your group will need to work together in order to agree upon the town construction and people. Here are some steps to follow:

1. Name your town.
2. Use the space below to draw a map of your town. Label the buildings.
3. Name the people who live in your town (approximately 25).
4. Mark each person on the map, perhaps with a number code.
5. Choose a date and time. Tell what 10 of the townspeople are doing at that particular minute.

Town Name

Geography: Manhattan

Here is a map of Manhattan. Find each of the following locations on the map. Circle or highlight them with a yellow marking pen.

- 82nd Street
- Fifth Avenue
- Upper East Side
- Carl Schurz Park
- East River

Brainstorm a list of other well known New York landmarks. Label them on the map. How far are they from Harriet's neighborhood?

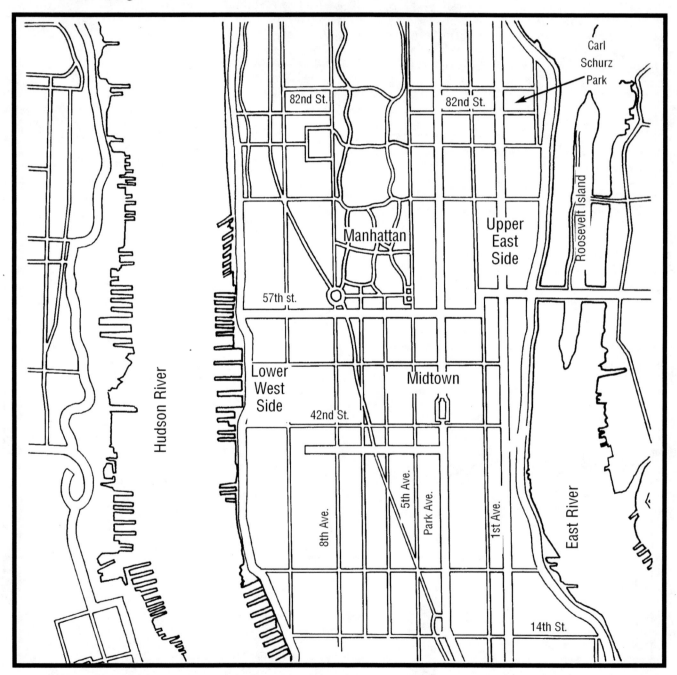

Challenge: In which direction is Far Rockaway? Pencil in an arrow pointing to Far Rockaway's direction on the map.

My Day

Harriet likes to lead her life with strict precision in regard to times and events. Do you have a regular schedule for your weekdays? In the space below, keep a schedule of one weekday in your life. ("Wake up" and "Go to bed" have been written in for you. You will need to write in all of the other things you do in your day. Use additional paper if necessary.) Once completed, compare this schedule to other weekdays to see how closely you match up from day to day.

Event	Time
Wake up	
Go to bed	

Quiz Time

1. On the back of this page, list three major events from this section of the book.

2. What does Harriet carry so that she can be prepared for blending into the scenery while spying?

   _____

3. Harriet thinks she would be bored to death if she were what?

   _____

4. Harriet wonders if everybody is a "different person when they are with somebody else." Whose behavior makes her wonder this? What behavior does that person exhibit?

   _____

   _____

5. What was Mr. Waldenstein's profession before becoming a delivery boy?

   _____

6. What is Ole Golly's first name? What is Mr. Waldenstein's first name?

   _____

   _____

7. Where and in what does Harriet ride when she goes out with Ole Golly and Mr. Waldenstein?

   _____

8. To what two places do Ole Golly and Mr. Waldenstein take Harriet?

   _____

9. Why does Mrs. Welsch fire Ole Golly?

   _____

   _____

10. After Ole Golly leaves, Harriet writes, ". . . there's a funny little hole in me that wasn't there before. . ." What is she talking about?

    _____

    _____

    _____

    _____

Make a Birdcage

Harrison Withers spends his time making intricate and beautiful birdcages. You can make a birdcage, too, by following these directions.

Materials:

- craft sticks
- craft glue
- heavy corrugated cardboard
- brass fastener
- ruler
- scissors

Directions:

1. Trace a square onto the cardboard, using the ruler for a straight edge. The square will be the base of your birdcage.

2. Cut the square from the cardboard.

3. Glue craft sticks lengthwise along the perimeter of the cardboard square to completely border it.

4. At approximately 1.5" (3.75 cm) intervals, glue craft sticks perpendicular to the base all the way around the perimeter.

5. At approximately 3" (7.5 cm) intervals, glue craft sticks perpendicular to the vertical craft sticks all the way across their lengths.

6. Keep building and gluing in this way, making the birdcage as tall as you would like and leaving an opening of about 5" (12.5 cm) square on one side. This will be the doorway.

7. Cut a door from cardboard 5" (12.5 cm) square.

8. Poke the brass fastener through the door near the left edge. Spin it in place. Open the stems of the fastener. This will make the door latch.

9. Complete the door by gluing craft sticks side by side on the front of the cardboard, leaving enough room for the fastener to turn. This will finish the door.

10. Make a door hinge by gluing two cardboard tabs near the right top side of the door, front and back, extending halfway off the edge of the right side. Do the same for the bottom door hinge. Gently bend the hinges by moving the door back and forth. This will make the hinges bend easily.

11. Attach the door to the birdcage by gluing the cardboard door hinges (one tab on each side of the door frame) to the birdcage door opening. When the door is closed, turn the fastener so that the stem crosses the left side of the doorway. This will latch the door.

12. Cut a cardboard square slightly larger than the base. Cover it with craft sticks. Glue the roof to the top of the cage. (In order to make a peaked roof, you will need to cut the cardboard into four triangles and glue them together into a peak. Cover them with sticks and glue the roof to the cage.)

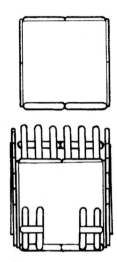

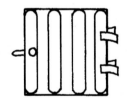

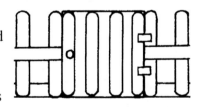

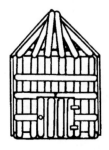

Co-operEggtions

Sport's most-used recipes involve eggs. In small groups, collect all the egg recipes you can find. (You can ask your parents, relatives, friends, and neighbors. You might even invent one of your own!) As a group, write each of the recipes and add some interesting illustrations. Form the recipes into a group book. Color and cut out the graphic below for your recipe book cover. Add the names of your group members in the empty space.

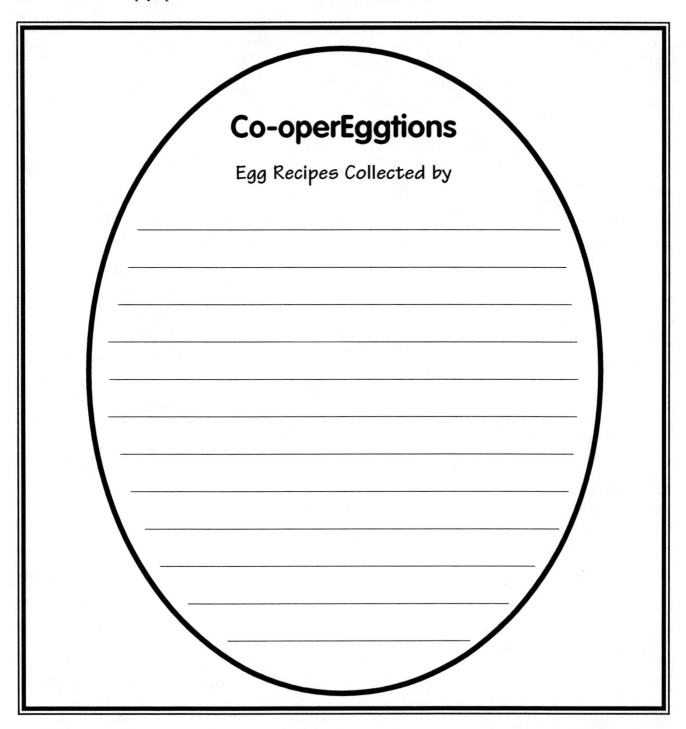

Challenge: As a group, make one of your egg recipes for the class. Combine the recipes for a classroom egg feast.

Chemistry: Experimenting

Janie Gibbs is quite a scientist. Her specialty is chemistry, the science that deals with the properties, compositions, and transformations of substances. Here is a chemical experiment to try in your classroom. It concerns acid and its ability to weaken minerals. It is known that water sometimes mixes with other elements to make a weak acid which can wear away at the minerals in some kinds of rocks to change the rock's hardness. What will be the effect of a weak acid (vinegar) on an eggshell (which contains the mineral calcium)? Follow these steps. (**Note:** When handling raw eggs, be sure to wash your hands and all surfaces that come in contact with them.)

Materials:

- 1 raw egg
- white distilled vinegar
- spoon
- clear cup larger than the egg

Directions:

1. Carefully place the egg in the cup.
2. Cover the egg completely with vinegar.
3. Wait two days. Do not touch the egg. (This may cause the shell to crack and allow the yolk to escape, thus altering the experiment.)
4. After two days, remove the egg with the spoon. Touch it gently. What has happened to the shell?

My Ole Golly

Miss Golly, known to Harriet as Ole Golly, is Harriet's primary caretaker. She sees to Harriet's needs and teaches Harriet a great deal about life. Who in your life do you think has been your most significant caretaker? Describe that person by responding to the prompts below.

My Ole Golly's name: _____

How long I have known him/her: _____

The most important things he/she has done for me: _____

_____

_____

The most important things he/she has taught me: _____

_____

_____

What he/she has meant to me: _____

_____

_____

_____

_____

_____

_____

Quiz Time

1. On the back of this page, list three major events from this section of the book.

2. Name a difference Harriet feels in the house since Ole Golly went away.

    _____

    _____

3. Who likes to watch kids' programs and science shows?

    _____

4. What is Harriet's part in the school pageant?

    _____

5. What is Fabio Dei Santi's new job?

    _____

6. What horrible thing happens to Harrison Withers at the end of chapter eight?

    _____

7. How do Harriet's parents feel when they see her writing in her notebook and she refuses to share it with them?

    _____

    _____

8. What happens to Harriet during her visit inside Mrs. Plumber's house in chapter nine?

    _____

    _____

9. What is the one essential thing about spies, according to Harriet?

    _____

10. What happens in Harriet's nightmare?

    _____

    _____

    _____

Inanimation

Miss Berry believes that through creative dance, a person can portray any object in existence. As a class, brainstorm a list of inanimate objects. (The list has been started for you, with the items named in the book.) Each student can choose one item from the list and create his or her own dance to portray that object for the class. The class will then guess which object from the list is being portrayed.

bathtub

celery

chair

cranberries

gravy

onion

pea

squash

table

turkey (cooked)

Pageant

Harriet's class must work together to create an act for the school Christmas pageant. Create a pageant for your classroom, composed of skits performed by various groups. Set a date for your classroom pageant and then follow these directions.

- Divide into groups of four or five.

- Each group must agree upon an act for that group to perform for the class. Nominate ideas and vote on them in the same way it is done in the book. You may choose any sort of act, such as a dance, song, skit, puppet show, or magic show. Summarize your ideas below.

- Once you have determined your act, work together to decide what costumes, props, sets, etc., you will need to perform the act. List the materials you need below.

- Work together to gather all necessary materials.

- If your act requires a script, write it.

- Cast all parts.

- Rehearse your act several times.

- Have a final rehearsal or two with costumes and props.

- Perform for the classroom pageant!

Here is a summary of the act our group has chosen to perform.

_____

_____

_____

_____

_____

The costumes, props, sets, and other materials we will need are as follows:

_____

_____

_____

_____

_____

Biology: The Brain

Harriet wonders about the appearance of the brain. Is everyone's brain alike, or does each brain reflect a person's outside appearance?

Below is a diagram of a normal human brain. In the word box are the names of some of the important places in and around the brain. Label each part correctly, using the words provided. Then, color the areas as indicated in the parentheses.

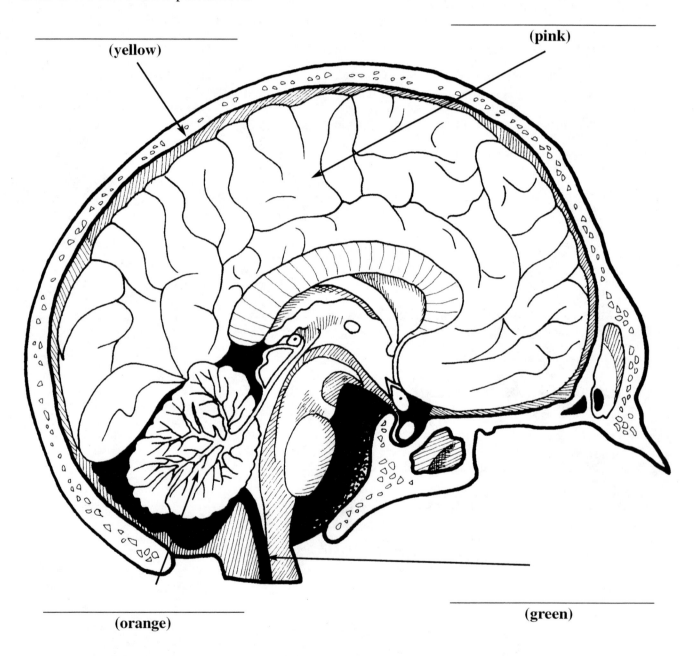

(yellow)

(pink)

(orange)

(green)

Word Box	
cerebellum	skull
cerebrum	spinal cord

Choices

Harriet refuses to portray an onion in her class Christmas dance. However, her refusal is ignored. After all, as Sport tells her, "You can't quit. This is a SCHOOL." Sometimes, people must do or not do things because of the rules. Other times, they make their own choices. Of course, sometimes they choose to break the rules, which may be wrong or right, depending on the circumstances.

In the columns below, make two lists, writing as many things as you can think of. In the first column, write the rules you must follow in your life. In the second column, write the things that you can decide for yourself.

Rules	Choices
Completing my homework on time	Which clothes to wear to school

Quiz Time

1. On the back of this page, list three major events from this section of the book.

2. How does Harriet lose her notebook?

   _____

3. The day after her notebook is found, what is stolen from Harriet?

   _____

4. What does Harriet write in her notebook in big letters like those when she first learned to write?

   _____

5. Harriet decides that when she becomes a spy, she will learn everyone's secrets and tell them to their enemies. How does she hope people will feel about her then?

   _____

6. What does her mother do that helps Harriet to feel better?

   _____

   _____

7. Who lets Harriet know that the other children have a plan?

   _____

   _____

8. What do the children build in Rachel's yard?

   _____

9. What does Rachel do to Harriet in the classroom?

   _____

10. What do the children do while Harriet is writing in the park?

    _____

    _____

Make a Cake

Harriet and her friends love to eat homemade cake. You can make a basic chocolate cake by following the directions below. Afterwards, serve the cake to your friends with a glass of milk.

Ingredients:

- 2 cups (500 mL) cake flour
- 2 cups (500 mL) sugar
- 1 teaspoon (5 mL) soda
- 1 teaspoon (5 mL) salt

- $\frac{1}{2}$ teaspoon (2.5 mL) baking powder
- $\frac{3}{4}$ cup (185 mL) water
- $\frac{3}{4}$ cup (185 mL) buttermilk
- $\frac{1}{2}$ cup (125 mL) shortening

- 2 eggs
- 1 teaspoon (5 mL) vanilla
- 4 ounces (115 g) melted unsweetened chocolate, cooled

Materials:

- 2 – 9" (22.5 cm) baking pans
- large spoon or rubber spatula

- oven
- large mixing bowl
- electric mixer

- serving plate
- knife

Preparations:

1. Heat the oven to 350°F (180°C).

2. Grease and flour the baking pans.

3. Place all ingredients into the mixing bowl.

4. Mix the ingredients for 30 seconds on a low speed and 3 minutes on a high speed.

5. Pour the batter evenly into the two pans.

6. Place the pans in the preheated oven and bake for 30–35 minutes or until a toothpick inserted gently in the center of each cake comes out clean.

7. Cool the cakes for fifteen minutes and then remove them from the pans.

8. Cool completely and frost or serve warm without frosting. Cut into slices.

Our Clubhouse

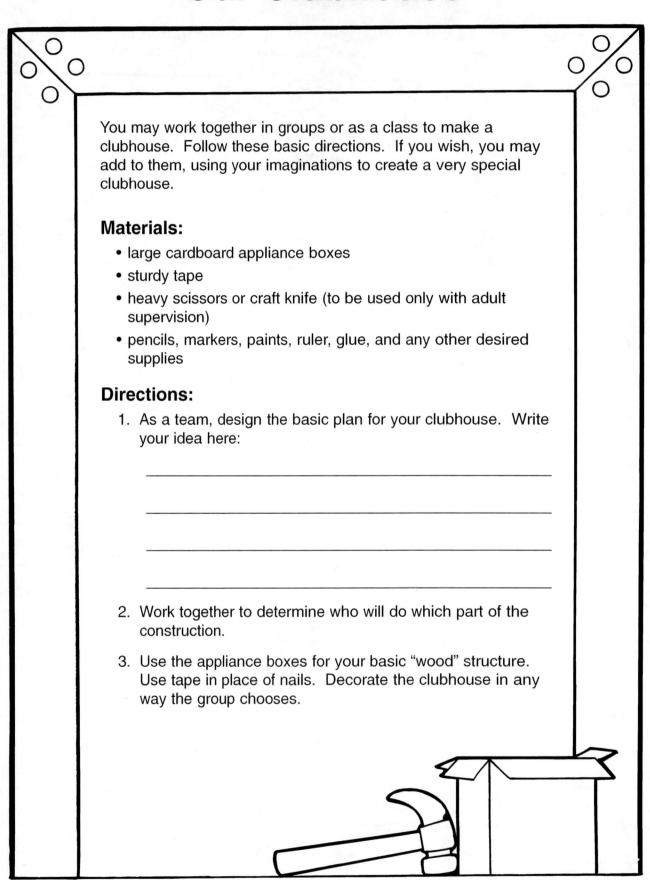

You may work together in groups or as a class to make a clubhouse. Follow these basic directions. If you wish, you may add to them, using your imaginations to create a very special clubhouse.

Materials:

- large cardboard appliance boxes
- sturdy tape
- heavy scissors or craft knife (to be used only with adult supervision)
- pencils, markers, paints, ruler, glue, and any other desired supplies

Directions:

1. As a team, design the basic plan for your clubhouse. Write your idea here:

    _____

    _____

    _____

    _____

2. Work together to determine who will do which part of the construction.

3. Use the appliance boxes for your basic "wood" structure. Use tape in place of nails. Decorate the clubhouse in any way the group chooses.

Math: Harriet's Favorites

Harriet hates math, but there are many other things she really likes. Make a list of the things Harriet likes and use them to make up a variety of math problems that even Harriet might enjoy. Challenge others in your class to solve your math equations.

Here is an example:

Harriet eats one tomato sandwich a day. If one tomato sandwich uses $\frac{1}{3}$ of a tomato, how many tomatoes are used in 4 weeks?

My Memoirs

After her first notebook is taken, Harriet begins writing her memoirs in her new notebook. She starts with her earliest memory. In the space below, tell about your earliest memory. Describe it in as much detail as you can. If you are willing, share your memory with the class.

Quiz Time

1. On the back of this page, list three major events from this section of the book.

2. What does Harriet do to Laura Peters out of meanness?

   _____

3. What causes the cook to nearly quit?

   _____

   _____

4. Whose name does Harriet repeat as she lies in her room?

   _____

5. What does Harriet do when her father comes into her room at night?

   _____

6. What sort of doctor is Dr. Wagner?

   _____

7. What wonderful thing happens to Sport's father?

   _____

8. In Ole Golly's letter to Harriet, what two things does she say she must do if her notebooks are ever read?

   _____

   _____

9. What school assignment is given to Harriet by Miss Whitehead and Miss Elson?

   _____

10. What does Harriet do that causes Sport and Janie to seek her out once again?

   _____

   _____

Mirror Image

Harriet begins to have greater compassion and understanding when she imagines what it is like to be other people, for example, Sport and Janie. She tries to put herself in their shoes.

Activity

Part One

Privately think of someone you know. Silently, imagine yourself as that person right now. Imagine everything about how that person looks and then imagine that this is how you look. Take each feature and bit of coloring on that person and think of it as belonging to you. Then, think about the sorts of things that person does with his or her day. Imagine what some of his or her thoughts, worries, and pleasures might be. Try to understand what it might be like to be that person. Do you feel a greater understanding or sympathy for him or her?

Part Two

Partner up with someone in the classroom. The two of you will need to stand face to face as though you were the mirror image of the other. One person will be A and the other will be B. First A will make slow and careful movements with his/her face and/or body. B will try to copy them exactly, just as a mirror would. Do not speak. Pay very careful attention to your partner. After two or three minutes, your teacher will call "time," and A will then copy B's motions for five minutes. How well do you do this? Are you able to focus completely on the other person? Do your own concerns and feelings get in the way? Discuss as a class what this experience is like for each of you. How thoroughly can you "be" someone else?

Extension: Just for fun, see if anyone in the class is able to do any celebrity impersonations.

Little Joe and the Children

Throughout the novel, Little Joe Dei Santi takes food from the family market and gives it to the poor children who come to his back door. In this section of the book, his mother finds out what he does, and though she acts angry, she hands the children even more food. The Dei Santi's seem to care a great deal about making sure the children have plenty to eat.

You can get involved in a very similar way in helping to feed a family who needs your help. First, you will need to call local charitable organizations and churches. They will likely be able to connect you to a family in need of assistance. Next, determine, as a class, the kind of assistance you can provide. Work together to gather food and, perhaps, clothing. Decorate boxes in which to place the donated items. Arrange for a delivery of the goods, along with a special note from the class, wishing the family well. If possible, the exchange can be made in person.

This activity can be continued on a regular basis, perhaps each month or school quarter, each time with a different family. The students will learn the pleasures and rewards of helping others in need.

As an extension of this same idea, ask the students to brainstorm other ways in which they can be of assistance to the community. Give them the form below on which to jot down their ideas. Come back as a class and pool the ideas, voting on the ones you wish to carry out.

In order to help the community, our class can . . .

_____

_____

_____

_____

_____

_____

_____

_____

_____

Language Arts: Class Page

Harriet rejoices when she is made editor of the sixth-grade page in the school newspaper. Using the form below, write a news page reporting the news for your own class. Share your news page with the class. Did everyone choose similar stories to tell? What are the most common stories? How do the news stories differ?

Note: There should be no gossip or personal information revealed.

_____ – **Grade Page**

by _____

_____   _____

_____   _____

_____   _____

_____   _____

_____   _____

_____   _____

_____   _____

_____   _____

_____   _____

_____   _____

My Notebook

Harriet feels lost without her notebook. Its presence seems to help her think. Her thoughts come quickly and easily when she has some place to record them.

Try keeping your own notebook for one week. Take it everywhere you go. Write down your thoughts about your experiences, people you meet, feelings, and so on. You will not need to share this information. Your teacher will only look to see that it is complete.

Directions for making your notebook: Decorate and cut out the notebook cover below. Glue it to a piece of 9" x 12" (23 cm x 30 cm) construction paper. Attach several sheets of notebook paper behind the cover and add a construction paper back cover. Staple or glue your book pages together.

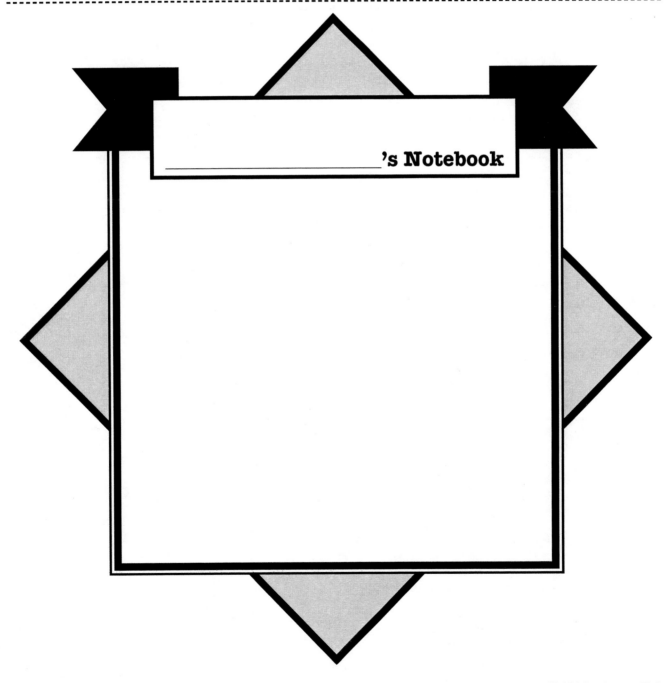

_____'s Notebook

Any Questions?

When you finished reading *Harriet the Spy*, did you have any questions that were left unanswered? Write your questions here.

_____

_____

_____

_____

_____

_____

_____

_____

_____

_____

_____

_____

_____

Work in groups or by yourself to prepare possible answers for some or all of the questions you have asked above and those written below. When you have finished your predictions, share your ideas with the class.

- Will Harriet ever see Ole Golly again?

- Will Harriet be a writer when she grows up?

- Will Harriet, Janie, and Sport continue to be friends into adulthood?

- What will happen to each of the people and families on Harriet's spy route?

Book Report Ideas

There are many ways to report on a book once it has been read. After you have finished reading *Harriet the Spy*, choose a method of reporting on it that appeals to you. It may be an idea of your own or one of the suggestions mentioned below.

The Eyes Have It

Do a visual report by making a model of a scene from the story. Draw or sculpt a likeness of one or more of the characters or craft an important symbol or object from the book.

Time Capsule

Provide people in the future with reasons to read *Harriet the Spy*. Inside a time-capsule-shaped design, neatly write your reasons. You may "bury" your capsule after you have shared it with the class.

Come to Life!

A size-appropriate group prepares a scene from the story for dramatization, acts it out, and relates the significance of the scene to the entire book. Costumes and props will add to the dramatization.

Into the Future

Predict what might happen if *Harriet the Spy* were to continue. You may write it as a story in narrative form, a dramatic script, or do a visual display.

Guess Who or What

This report takes the form of "Twenty Questions." The reporter starts by giving a series of clues, one by one, about a character from the story. The clues are general at first and gradually become more specific. After each clue, someone may try to guess the character. After all the clues, if the subject cannot be guessed, the reporter may tell the class. The reporter then does the same for an event from the book and then for an important object or symbol.

A Character Comes to Life

Suppose one of the characters from *Harriet the Spy* came to life and walked into your classroom or home? This report gives the character's point of view as she or he sees, hears, feels, and experiences the world in which you live.

Sales Talk

This is an advertisement to "sell" *Harriet the Spy* to one or more specific groups. You decide on a group to target and the sales campaign you will use. Include some kind of graphics in your presentation, as well as reasons you think your "product" is worthwhile.

Coming Attraction

Harriet the Spy is about to be made into a movie, and you have been chosen to design the promotional poster. Include the title and author of the book and a listing of the main characters and the contemporary actors who will portray them. Draw a scene from the book and write a paragraph synopsis of the story that will make audiences want to see the movie. (**Note:** This must be original and in no way a duplicate of the promotional poster for the 1996 film.)

Literary Interview

This report is done in pairs. One student will pretend to be a character from the story and steep him/herself completely in that character's persona. The other student will play the role of a radio or television interviewer, trying to provide the audience with insights into the character's personality and life that the audience most wants to know. It is the responsibility of the partners to create meaningful questions and appropriate answers.

Research Ideas

Describe three things that you read in *Harriet the Spy* that you would like to learn more about.

1. _____

   _____

2. _____

   _____

3. _____

   _____

As you read *Harriet the Spy*, you encountered many literary characters and true-life figures, including scientists, artists, writers, world leaders, entertainers, and more. To increase your understanding of the book, try to find out more about these characters and people.

Work in groups to research one or more of the people/characters who are listed below. Share your findings with the rest of the class in any appropriate format for oral presentation.

- Henry James
- Paul Gauguin
- Fyodor Dostoevsky
- Zeus
- Apollo
- Athena
- Elizabeth Arden
- Johann Wolfgang von Goethe
- Louis Pasteur
- Grigory Rasputin
- Thomas Wolfe
- William Faulkner
- Puck
- Willie Mays
- Mickey Mantle
- Oskar Kokoschka
- Dr. Jekyll and Mr. Hyde

- Paul Newman
- Monsieur and Madame Curie
- Albert Einstein
- Sir Isaac Newton
- Mata Hari
- William Wordsworth
- William Cowper
- Ralph Waldo Emerson
- Shirley MacLaine
- Dr. Kildare
- Ben Casey
- Sergeant York
- Konstantin Stanislavsky
- Adolph Hitler
- Good Humor Man
- General Eisenhower
- John Keats

Book of Quotes

Through Ole Golly, Harriet is exposed to the wisdom of great writers throughout time. Ole Golly seems to have an appropriate quote handy for every occasion. To culminate your reading of *Harriet the Spy*, put together a class quote book. On the pages that follow are listed a variety of significant topics. Each class member should look for and find a published quote pertaining to at least six of these topics. Ask parents, friends, relatives, and neighbors for their ideas. Be sure to quote the text exactly as it is printed. Give an appropriate reference for the author or source. Write the quotes in the spaces that follow. Cut out and arrange all the quotes together into a class book, designing a cover for the book as a group. As an extension, display one quote a day on the class chalkboard or bulletin board and discuss its meaning and veracity.

— —

Adulthood

— —

Anger

— —

Art

Book of Quotes *(cont.)*

— —
Children

— —
Dreams

— —
Family

— —
Forgiveness

— —
Friendship

Book of Quotes _(cont.)

_ _ _ _ _ _ _ _ _ _ _ _ _ _ _ _ _ _ _

Future

_ _ _ _ _ _ _ _ _ _ _ _ _ _ _ _ _ _ _

Goals

_ _ _ _ _ _ _ _ _ _ _ _ _ _ _ _ _ _ _

Growing Up

_ _ _ _ _ _ _ _ _ _ _ _ _ _ _ _ _ _ _

Happiness

_ _ _ _ _ _ _ _ _ _ _ _ _ _ _ _ _ _ _

Hope

Book of Quotes (cont.)

— — — — — — — — — — — — — — — — — — — —

Justice

— — — — — — — — — — — — — — — — — — — —

Life

— — — — — — — — — — — — — — — — — — — —

Loss

— — — — — — — — — — — — — — — — — — — —

Love

— — — — — — — — — — — — — — — — — — — —

Peace

Book of Quotes (cont.)

— — — — — — — — — — — — — — — — — — —
Prosperity

— — — — — — — — — — — — — — — — — — —
Sharing

— — — — — — — — — — — — — — — — — — —
Sorrow

— — — — — — — — — — — — — — — — — — —
Truth

— — — — — — — — — — — — — — — — — — —
Work

Objective Test and Essay

Matching: Match the descriptions of the characters with their names by placing the letters before the corresponding numbers.

_____	1. Harriet M. Welsch	a. man who loves cats
_____	2. Ole Golly	b. Harriet's best friend
_____	3. Sport Rocque	c. rich woman who fears she is bedridden
_____	4. Janie Gibbs	d. delivery man who was once a jeweler
_____	5. Harrison Withers	e. Harriet's nurse and teacher
_____	6. Little Joe Dei Santi	f. shy and insecure girl
_____	7. Agatha Plumber	g. girl who manipulates to be in charge of everything
_____	8. George Waldenstein	h. girl who wants to be a writer
_____	9. Miss Berry	i. girl who wants to be a scientist
_____	10. Marion Hawthorne	j. man who helps Harriet's parents to help her
_____	11. Beth Ellen Hansen	k. school dance teacher
_____	12. Dr. Wagner	l. young man who gives food to poor children

True or False: Answer true or false in the blanks below.

_____ 1. Harriet is eleven years old.

_____ 2. Ole Golly's first name is Margery.

_____ 3. Harriet is never caught while spying.

_____ 4. Harriet takes revenge on her classmates after they shun her.

_____ 5. Sport forgives Harriet.

Short Answer: Write a brief response to each question in the space provided.

1. What is one of the things that Harriet learns from Ole Golly?_____

2. How does Harriet feel about Sport? _____

3. How does Harriet feel about the Robinsons? _____

4. How does Harrison Withers find happiness again?_____

5. Name one thing Mr. and Mrs. Welsch do to help Harriet. _____

Essay: Respond to the following on the back of this paper.

Describe in detail one person or family on Harriet's spy route. What significant things does that person or family do? How does Harriet feel about him/her/them?

Response

Explain the meaning of these quotations from *Harriet the Spy*. Support your ideas.

Chapter 1   *Harriet realized with a start that it was the first time she had ever seen Ole Golly look sad. She hadn't even known Ole Golly could be sad.*

Chapter 2   *"It won't do you a bit of good to know everything if you don't do anything with it."*

Chapter 3   *Little Joe went back to his eating. Harriet felt funny watching the scene.*

Chapter 4   *Because the Robinsons had only one problem. They thought they were perfect.*

Chapter 5   *Harriet hated more than anything else to be told by Ole Golly that she wasn't thinking.*

Chapter 6   *"Life was worth nothing. It was so much dust in my hands."*

Chapter 7   *I wonder if when you dream about somebody they dream about you.*

Chapter 8   *I mean do people look like that when they have <u>lost</u>?*

Chapter 9   *Harriet ran all the way home and all the way up to her room, where she flung herself on the bed and cried with all her might.*

Chapter 10   *They just looked and looked, and their eyes were the meanest eyes she had ever seen.*

Chapter 11   *I love myself.*

Chapter 12   *"I'm not playing! Who says I'm playing? I'm WORKING!"*

Chapter 13   *She sat very stupidly with a blank mind until finally "I feel different" came slowly into her head.*

Chapter 14   *I can't, she thought, live here.*

Chapter 15   *And, for some reason, as she walked home Harriet felt unaccountably happy.*

Chapter 16   *Now that things are back to normal I can get some real work done.*

Conversations

Work in size-appropriate groups to write and perform the conversations that might have occurred in one of the following situations. If you prefer, you may use your own conversation idea for characters from *Harriet the Spy*.

- Harriet and Ole Golly discuss Mrs. Golly. (2 people)

- Mrs. Golly and Ole Golly talk about Ole Golly's childhood. (2 people)

- Ole Golly tells Harriet about Mr. Waldenstein. (2 people)

- Little Joe and the children meet and talk. (4 or more people)

- Mr. and Mrs. Welsch discuss Harriet's negative behavior at home and school. (2 people)

- Mr. and Mrs. Welsch and Ole Golly meet after Ole Golly's marriage. (3 people)

- Ole Golly and Mr. Waldenstein meet when they are children. (2 people)

- Sport and Janie discuss their feelings about Harriet's comments in her notebook. (2 people)

- Sport, Janie, and Harriet meet as adults. (3 people)

- Harriet and Ole Golly meet at Harriet's college graduation. (2 people)

- Mr. Rocque and Harriet meet at a writers' convention. (2 people)

- Marion Hawthorne, Beth Ellen Hansen, Rachel Hennessey, Janie, Sport, and Harriet meet as adults. (6 people)

- The Boy with the Purple Socks and his mother talk about his life at school. (2 people)

- Sport and his father discuss their finances and future. (2 people)

- The Robinsons catch Harriet spying on them. (3 people)

- Harrison Withers catches Harriet spying on him. (2 people)

- Miss Berry, Miss Elson, Miss Dodge, and Miss Harris meet in the teacher's lounge. (4 people)

Answer Key

Page 11: Quiz Time

1. Responses will vary.

2. Responses will vary. Accept any reasonable descriptions.

3. Responses will vary. Accept any reasonable descriptions.

4. Harriet lives in New York City (Manhattan).

5. Harriet wants to be a writer. She is spying on people, making judgments about them, and writing about them in order to prepare for her career.

6. Sport wants to be a professional football player. For a backup choice, he would like to be an accountant (CPA).

7. Responses will vary. Accept any reasonable responses.

8. Responses will vary. Accept any reasonable responses.

9. Mrs. Plumber is the rich woman Harriet spies on by hiding in her dumbwaiter. Harriet observes many things about her in chapter 3. Accept any observations given in that chapter.

10. Responses will vary. Accept any reasonable responses.

Page 16: Quiz Time

1. Responses will vary.

2. Harriet carries a ball.

3. Harriet thinks she would be bored to death if she were perfect.

4. Ole Golly's behavior while around Mr. Waldenstein makes her wonder this.

5. Mr. Waldenstein was a jeweler.

6. Ole Golly's first name is Catherine, and Mr. Waldenstein's first name is George.

7. Harriet rides inside the storage compartment of Mr. Waldenstein's delivery bicycle.

8. Ole Golly and Mr. Waldenstein take Harriet to the movies and to the drugstore (for an egg cream).

9. Mrs. Welsch fires Ole Golly because, at midnight, she does not know where Harriet went or what she did.

10. Responses will vary. Accept any reasonable answers.

Page 21: Quiz Time

1. Responses will vary.

2. Responses will vary. Accept all applicable responses.

3. Janie Gibbs likes to watch kids' programs and science shows.

4. Harriet's part in the school pageant is an onion.

5. Fabio Dei Santi's new job is salesman.

6. Harrison Withers' cats have been taken away.

7. Harriet's parents feel left out and upset because Harriet used to confide in Ole Golly but will not share with them.

8. During her visit inside Mrs. Plumber's house in chapter 9, Harriet is caught inside the dumbwaiter and thrown out of the house.

9. The one essential thing about spies, according to Harriet, is that they not be caught.

10. Accept any descriptions of Harriet's nightmare that include the basics of Ole Golly as a bird and coming after Harriet.

Page 24: Biology: The Brain

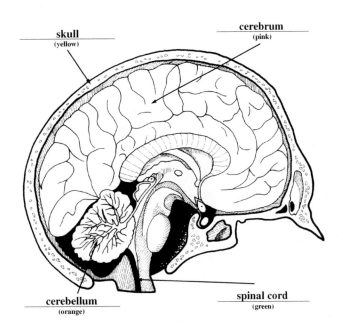

skull (yellow)

cerebrum (pink)

cerebellum (orange)

spinal cord (green)

Answer Key

Page 26: Quiz Time

1. Responses will vary.
2. Harriet loses her notebook while playing tag.
3. Harriet's tomato sandwich is stolen.
4. Harriet writes "EVERYBODY HATES ME" in her notebook.
5. Harriet hopes people will feel petrified.
6. Harriet's mother hugs her.
7. Rachel lets Harriet know that the other children have a plan.
8. The children build a clubhouse called The Spy Catcher Club.
9. Rachel pours a bottle of ink on Harriet.
10. The children have a Spy Catcher Club parade right past Harriet.

Page 29: Math: Harriet's Favorites

9 $\frac{1}{3}$ tomatoes

Page 31: Quiz Time

1. Responses will vary.
2. Harriet cuts a length of Laura Peters' hair.
3. The cook nearly quits because Harriet runs into her after school each day, and she also stomps to flatten the cook's cake. (Either answer is acceptable.)
4. Harriet repeats Ole Golly's name.
5. Harriet throws a shoe at her father.
6. Dr. Wagner is a psychologist or a psychiatrist.
7. Sport's father sells his book for publication.
8. Ole Golly tells Harriet that she must apologize and lie if her notebooks are read.
9. Harriet is made the editor of the sixth-grade page in the school newspaper.
10. Harriet prints a retraction concerning her comments in her notebook.

Page 44: Objective Test and Essay

Matching

1. h
2. e
3. b
4. i
5. a
6. l
7. c
8. d
9. k
10. g
11. f
12. j

True or False

1. true
2. false
3. false
4. true
5. true

Short Answer

1. Answers will vary.
2. Answers will vary.
3. Answers will vary. Basically, she finds them self-absorbed, boring, and silly.
4. He gets a new kitten.
5. Answers will vary.

Essay

Accept all reasonable responses.

Page 45: Response

Accept all reasonable and well-supported responses and explanations.

Page 46: Conversations

Perform the conversations in class. Ask students to respond to the conversations in several different ways such as, "Are the conversations realistic?" or, "Are the words the characters are saying in keeping with their personalities?"